Written by Clive Gifford.
Illustrations by Steve James.
Cover artwork based on designs by Thy Bui.

First published in Great Britain in 2022 by Red Shed, part of Farshore

An imprint of HarperCollins*Publishers*
1 London Bridge Street, London SE1 9GF
www.farshore.co.uk

HarperCollins*Publishers*
1st Floor, Watermarque Building, Ringsend Road
Dublin 4, Ireland

Copyright © HarperCollins*Publishers* Limited 2022

ISBN 978 0 00 856219 9

Printed and bound in the UK using 100% Renewable Electricity at CPI Group (UK) Ltd.

001

A CIP catalogue record for this title is available from the British Library.

MIX
Paper | Supporting
responsible forestry
FSC™ C007454

This book is produced from independently certified FSC™ paper
to ensure responsible forest management.

For more information visit: www.harpercollins.co.uk/green

AMAZING PUZZLES & QUIZZES FOR EVERY 9 YEAR OLD

RED SHED

Have fun cracking clues and tackling quizzes with this puzzle book!

You'll find loads of fun questions and exciting brain teasers to challenge yourself with – or you can test your friends and family for hours of fun together!

Along the way, you'll find a mix of all sorts of puzzles – spot the difference, anagrams, quizzes, mazes and more. Each puzzle has instructions at the top of the page that tell you what you need to do. Once you've got your answer, or if you get stuck, head to the back of the book to check the solution.

Lets get started!

Spot the Pair: Terrific Tigers

Only one of the labelled images on this page is identical to this tiger – all of the rest have small differences.

Can you work out which image is an exact match?

a)

b)

c)

d)

e)

Answers on page 75

Human Body

1. The smallest bone in your body is just 2–3mm long and shares its name with part of a horse's saddle. What's it called?

a) Ulna   b) Patella   c) Stirrup

2. What part of your body weighs about one fiftieth of your total weight but uses one fifth of all your energy?

a) Heart   b) Lungs   c) Brain

3. You have 2–5 million glands found all across your body that release which particular substance?

a) Snot   b) Sweat   c) Saliva

Answers on page 75

Anagrams: Football

These **five football terms** have all had their letters muddled up. Can you unscramble the capital letters on each line to reveal a football-themed word that completes the sentence? Where a term has more than one word, each word is scrambled separately.

If you get them all right, the first letters of each term spell out an **additional football term**!

After the rain, the DRGONU was very soft.

He scored, but the referee said it was EDFFISO.

The team raced forward in KATCTA, keen to score a goal.

She ran quickly over the ELNI.

The players went abroad for an NNNAERILATTIO match.

We scored, but the other team soon UEQEZADLI.

Long Lunch

Solve the maths puzzles to reveal the answers
to these questions! Start with the number at the top,
and apply each mathematical equation in turn,
working down the chain.

I. **The world's longest hot dog was longer than
a football pitch in length – but what did it measure
in total, to the nearest metre?**

50

×2

−20

−8

÷12

−4

×100

+4

?

Answers on page 76

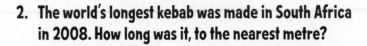

2. The world's longest kebab was made in South Africa in 2008. How long was it, to the nearest metre?

17

−2

÷3

×4

×100

+50

−3

?

BONUS SIDE ORDER

1. For a time in the 1800s, tomato ketchup was sold as a medicine, not a sauce. True or false?

2. The largest number of different types of cheese put on a single pizza is 124. True or false?

Children's Classics

1. Which well-known character journeyed through the looking glass, where she met the Cheshire Cat and the Queen of Hearts?

a) Alice **b)** Jemima **c)** Roberta

2. In *The Lion, The Witch and The Wardrobe* by C S Lewis, what was the name of the lion?

a) Rex **b)** Aslan **c)** Rory

3. Which author wrote *The Twits, Matilda* and *Fantastic Mr Fox*?

a) Roald Dahl
b) Jacqueline Wilson
c) Maurice Sendak

4. Some letters have been deleted from the name of a well-known Danish writer below, who is best-known for his fairy tales. Can you work out who it is?

H[redacted]N[redacted] [redacted]H[redacted]I[redacted]T[redacted]A[redacted]
A[redacted]D[redacted]R[redacted]E[redacted]

Answers on page 77

Coral Reef Maze

Can you help the baby fish find a path through this maze from the start to the finish?

It's Pants!

Can you solve the maths puzzles to answer these questions all about pants? Start with the number at the top, and apply each mathematical equation in turn, working down the chain. Try to do them in your head!

I. **The world's largest underpants were made in Egypt in 2018. What was their waist size, to the nearest metre?**

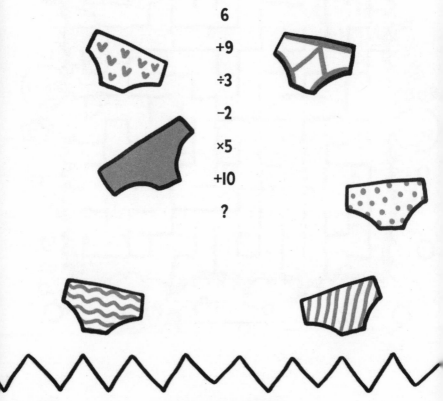

6

+9

÷3

−2

×5

+10

?

Answers on page 78

2. **Australian Steve Jacobs holds the record for the most pairs of pants worn one on top of another at the same time. How many pairs of pants did he manage to put on?**

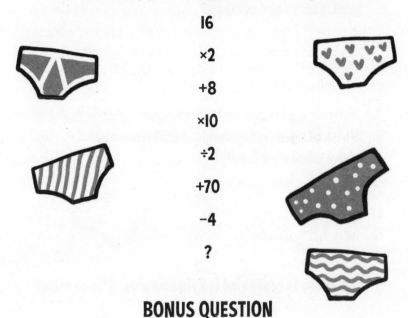

16

×2

+8

×10

÷2

+70

−4

?

BONUS QUESTION

King Henry VIII was buried with his 12 favourite pairs of underpants. True or false?

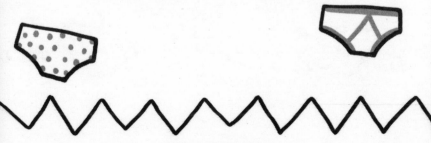

Musical Mischief

I. What sort of musician sits on a stool and plays toms, snares and cymbals?

a) A saxophonist
b) A drummer
c) A keyboard player

2. Which of these instruments is NOT a member of the woodwind family?

a) French horn
b) Bassoon
c) Flute

3. Ed Sheeran's real name is Kyle Edwards. True or false?

4. There's a popular heavy metal band in Finland for children called Hevisaurus, whose band members often dress as dinosaurs to perform. True or false?

Answers on page 79

Broken Pieces

Pickles the cat keeps pushing crockery off the shelf! Some of these vases are broken beyond repair, but can you find the two pieces that fit together from the pieces below? The completed vase will match the one on the shelf below.

a) b) c) d) e) f) g) h)

Toilet Time

1. **The average person visits the toilet approximately how many times each year?**

   a) 950   **b)** 2,500   **c)** 10,000

2. **The Sultan of Brunei's palace in south-east Asia has more than 250 bathrooms. True or false?**

3. **What did the ancient Romans use instead of loo paper in public toilets?**

   a) A sponge on a stick
   b) Corn cobs
   c) Clumps of grass
   and moss

Riddle Time: Who Am I?

Can you find the answer to this riddle
using the clues on each line?

My first is in FINGER and also in HAND,

My second is in SIDE but never in SEND,

My third is in GOAL but not in LOANS,

My fourth is in HOLE but not in LOOPED,

My fifth is at the start of TOMORROW.

What am I?
Turn the book upside-down for a hint . . .

I am a time when you usually sleep.

Magical Myths

I. Who was the Roman god of fire, volcanoes and metalworking?

a) Neptune   **b)** Vulcan   **c)** Blazius

2. Which calendar month gets its name from Janus, the Roman god of beginnings and endings?

a) January   **b)** June   **c)** July

3. In Greek mythology, which hero slayed the Minotaur?

a) Theseus
b) Jason
c) Achilles

Answers on page 80

Anagrams: Solar System

These **six things found in our Solar System** have all had their letters muddled up. Can you unscramble the capital letters on each line to reveal a word that completes the sentence?

The Roman god of war was RAMS.

A NESVU fly trap eats live insects to survive.

A EDREIOMTO is a lump of rock or metal that orbits the Sun.

UNRTSA is a planet with many rings around it.

On UNEETPN, some winds blow at over 1,000km/h!

It's thought that an RDATOISE hitting Earth caused dinosaurs to become extinct.

Unusual World

1. The jigsaw puzzle with the most pieces took 1,600 people to successfully piece it together in Vietnam in 2011. How many pieces do you think it had?

a) Around 3,000 pieces
b) Around 150,000 pieces
c) Around 550,000 pieces

2. In which country would you find big sculptures of bananas, prawns, pineapples and famous outlaw Ned Kelly as roadside attractions?

a) United States   b) Jamaica   c) Australia

3. In the Czech Republic, there is a chapel called *Sedlec Ossuary*, that is decorated with chandeliers and columns made of thousands of human skeletons. True or false?

History: True or False?

Can you work out which of these five statements
about history are true or false?

1. The Incas built a 40,000km network
   of roads but never used wheels.

2. All Vikings wore horned helmets.

3. In the Roman world, the year 46BCE was
   445 days long because of a change in calendars.

4. Ferdinand Magellan was
   the first sailor to sail all
   the way around the world.

5. Female gladiators,
   who were each called
   a gladiatrix, fought
   against each other
   in ancient Rome.

Creatures: True or False?

Can you work out which of these
four animal facts are true or false?

1. Octopuses have bright orange blood.

2. Dolphins sleep with one eye open.

3. Sea otters often attack dolphins and smaller sharks.

4. A flamingo's head has to be upside-down
   for it to be able to eat.

Answers on page 81

Riddle Time!

Can you work out the answers to these riddles?

1. Which is heavier, a tonne of rocks or a tonne of feathers?

2. What can be caught, but not thrown?

3. What can have three or four legs, but can't walk or run?

4. How many months of the year have 28 days?

5. What starts with an 'e', ends with an 'e', but only has one letter in it?

Answers on page 81

Dinner Time

1. **Which of these animals can catch and eat up to 3,000 insects in a night, despite its weight of less than 10g?**

a) A peregrine falcon
b) A natterjack toad
c) A common pipistrelle bat

2. **A mountain gorilla can spend around a quarter of its day eating. True or false?**

3. **People in Lopburi, Thailand, lay out a banquet for around 3,000 macaque monkeys each year. True or false?**

Answers on page 81

Make a Match: Sporting Stars

Can you match each first name in the left-hand column with one last name from the right-hand column to make the full names of **seven famous sportspeople**? Do you know what sports they are all known for?

Serena	Farah
Mo	Bolt
Lewis	Daley
Naomi	Williams
Tom	Hamilton
Usain	Biles
Simone	Osaka

Missing Words: From Spiders to Space

Each of the amazing facts on the next page is missing a single word. Can you select the one correct word from the list below to complete each of the six facts? To make it harder, there are two words that do not fit in any of the sentences.

Longest

Green

Shortest

Blue

Strongest

Brightest

Red

Smelliest

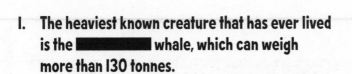

1. The heaviest known creature that has ever lived is the ▇▇▇▇▇▇ whale, which can weigh more than 130 tonnes.

2. The Darwin's bark spider spins the ▇▇▇▇▇▇ web of any spider in the world.

3. The football club Manchester United's nickname is the ▇▇▇▇▇▇ Devils.

4. The ▇▇▇▇▇▇ sausage ever recorded was made in Romania and stretched 62.75km.

5. The ▇▇▇▇▇▇ star (other than the Sun) that we can see from Earth is called Sirius.

6. The ▇▇▇▇▇▇ anaconda is the world's heaviest snake, weighing over 200kg.

Answers on page 82

Jigsaw: Cake Shop

Two pieces are missing from this jigsaw! Can you work out which of the puzzle pieces below fit exactly into the two empty spaces opposite to complete the image? The correct pieces need rotating.

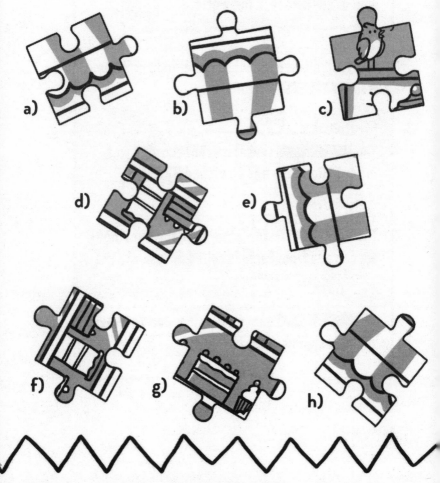

a)

b)

c)

d)

e)

f)

g)

h)

Awesome Astronomy

1. How old was Kathryn Aurora Gray in 2011 when she discovered a new supernova (an exploding star)?

a) 10   b) 14   c) 19

2. Which of these is the only known planet light enough to float in water, despite being the second-largest planet in our Solar System?

a) Venus   b) Saturn   c) Neptune

3. There's a big cloud of dust in space that astronomers think tastes of raspberries. True or false?

Answers on page 83

Change a Letter: From Cooking to Creatures

Altering just one single letter can create a word with a whole new meaning. Can you change a single letter in each of the following words to transform it into a different word, which answers the clue below it?

1. COT
A common pet

2. MATHS
Flying insects

3. GUTTER
A baking ingredient

4. FLOOR
What happens when a river overflows

5. FLEET
Snowy rain

6. BASK
An animal noise

Pirate Maze

Can you find a path through this maze from the start to the finish, to collect the treasure before the angry pirates find you?

Answers on page 84

Rugby Fun

1. **Which of these countries does NOT take part in the Six Nations rugby competition?**

a) France
b) Italy
c) Sweden

2. **If you are sin-binned in rugby, for how many minutes must you stay off the pitch?**

a) 2 minutes
b) 10 minutes
c) 25 minutes

3. **Which country's national rugby team are nicknamed the 'All Blacks', and perform a dance called a *haka* before every match?**

a) Wales
b) South Africa
c) New Zealand

Missing Numbers

Each of the amazing facts on the next page is missing a single number. Can you select the one correct number from the list below to complete each of the six facts? To make it harder, there are two numbers that don't fit into any of the sentences.

50

8

775

19

6,514

5

30

230

Answers on page 85

1. In the song The Twelve Days of Christmas, there are █████████ gold rings.

2. An octagon is a shape with ████████ sides.

3. An adult blue whale can grow up to around █████████ metres long.

4. The United States is divided into █████████ states.

5. Buckingham Palace in London contains █████████ rooms.

6. The Empire State Building in New York City has █████████ windows. That's a lot of window cleaning!

Answers on page 85

Follow the Line: Puzzled Pilots

These pilots have lost their planes! Can you follow the lines to work out which plane belongs with which pilot?

Answers on page 85

Movie Matters

1. Who has won the largest number of Oscars out of these three actors and filmmakers?

a) Emma Stone   **b)** Meryl Streep   **c)** Walt Disney

2. Which of these Britishs films has won the Oscar for best animated movie?

a) *Wallace and Gromit – The Curse of the Were-Rabbit*
b) *The Boxtrolls*
c) *Shaun the Sheep Movie*

3. In the *Monsters Inc* movie, 2.3 million individual hairs on the character of Sully all had to be animated. True or false?

Waterfalls

1. The world's tallest waterfall, Angel Falls, has a 979m drop – but in which continent is it found?

a) Asia
b) South America
c) Europe

2. In Antarctica, there is a waterfall called Blood Falls, whose waters run red like blood. True or false?

3. The first person to survive travelling over Niagara Falls in a barrel was a retired female schoolteacher. True or false?

Answers on page 85

Change a Letter: From Plants to Places

Altering just one single letter can create a word with a whole new meaning. Can you change a single letter in each of the following words to transform it into a different word, which answers the clue below it?

1. HOPE
A place where you live

2. CHIME
A herb

3. BOXES
Nocturnal, red-furred animals

4. MASTER
Quicker

5. TRAIN
An organ for thinking

6. CLEANING
A treeless area

Answers on page 86

Computer Gaming

1. **Which of these is a handheld computer gaming console?**

a) Game Boy   **b)** Xbox 360   **c)** Wii

2. **Which character that first appeared in the game Donkey Kong, has appeared in over 200 computer games since?**

a) Pikachu   **b)** Mario   **c)** Zelda

3. **What is the correct term for the style of computer game where you can move freely around and choose what tasks you complete?**

a) Worldshape
b) Sandbox
c) Stretchplay

Odd One Out: Fearless Flyers

All of the witches on this page are identical to one another – apart from one. Can you work out which image is different to the rest?

a)

b)

c)

d)

f)

e)

Answers on page 86

Fears and Phobias

1. **Some people suffer from coulrophobia. What is this a deep fear of?**

a) Clowns   **b)** Spiders   **c)** Shadows

2. **Film director Alfred Hitchcock suffered from ovaphobia, the fear of a certain kind of food. Which food was he scared of?**

a) Lemons   **b)** Eggs   **c)** Sausages

3. **People who suffer from arachnophobia are scared of what creature?**

a) Grasshoppers
b) Swans
c) Spiders

Anagrams: Emotions

Below is a list of **six emotions** that have been scrambled so their letters are out of order. Can you work out what the hidden emotions are? Each word has its first letter in bold, to help you.

SPS**H**PEIAN

SA**S**DNSE

GEN**R**A

SIUTS**D**G

MCNT**E**ITEEX

NNSU**C**OFIO

Ancient Egypt

1. **Tutankhamun's tomb contained six chariots, two thrones and how many walking sticks?**

a) 9   b) 24   c) 139

2. **Ancient Egyptian doctors used a range of different types of animal poo as medicine. True or false?**

3. **Which animal was kept by many ancient Egyptians as a pet, and was often mummified after its death?**

a) Cat   b) Gerbil   c) Goldfish

4. **The ancient Egyptian god Anubis was often shown with the head of which animal?**

a) Crocodile   b) Jackal   c) Parrot

Riddle Time: Who Am I?

Can you find the answer to this riddle using the clues on each line?

My first is in SIGHT and also in SMELL,

My second is in RINK and also in SKATE,

My third is in CHAIR but not in RANCH,

My fourth is always at the end of SEPTEMBER,

My fifth is in START but not in BARNS.

What am I?
Turn the book upside-down for a hint . . .

I am something to wear.

Peculiar Plants

1. **What highly-prized flavouring is made from certain parts of a type of crocus flower?**

a) Saffron
b) Vanilla
c) Tartar sauce

2. **Which fast-growing group of plants includes a species that can grow as much as 91cm in a single day? That's nearly the same length as a cricket bat!**

a) Conifer trees
b) Sunflower
c) Bamboo

3. **Low's pitcher plant feeds on the poo of little shrews. True or false?**

Answers on page 88

Super Science

1. **Which of these letters cannot be found in the periodic table of elements?**

a) B   **b)** Q   **c)** L

2. **What are scientists who study earthquakes called?**

a) Cytologists
b) Agronomists
c) Seismologists

3. **Which of these scientists discovered two radioactive elements, and was the first person to win two Nobel Prizes for science?**

a) Marie Curie
b) Albert Einstein
c) Louis Pasteur

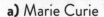

Answers on page 88

Smelly Stuff

1. **Approximately how much of your poo is made up of water?**

a) 52% b) 25% c) 75%

2. **The unpleasant scent of the zorilla (also known as the striped polecat) can be smelt from 800m away. True or false?**

3. **What smelly substance do flatologists study?**

a) Bad breath b) Rotting food c) Farts

Answers on page 88

Famous Figures

Can you rearrange these famous people from history into a timeline showing the order in which they lived? Start with the person who lived longest ago and end with the most recent. You might want to make some notes on a spare piece of paper.

Joan of Arc
French saint and military leader

William Shakespeare
English poet and playwright

Cleopatra VII
A ruler of ancient Egypt

Leonardo da Vinci
Italian artist and inventor

Marie Curie
Polish-French scientist

Maya Angelou
American poet and activist

Ingenious Engines: True or False?

Can you work out which of these statements about vehicles are true or false?

1. **The American Dream limousine car has a helipad, a swimming pool with a diving board, and a mini-golf course.**

2. **The world's fastest racing driver is Brittany Force. She reached 544.23km/h in a Top Fuel dragster race.**

3. **In 2016, a motorized fridge reached speeds of 140km/h in Germany.**

Answers on page 89

Waterways

1. **Which country has a canal running through it, that joins the Pacific and Atlantic Oceans?**

a) Sri Lanka   **b)** Brazil   **c)** Panama

2. **Which river runs through four capital cities including Vienna – more than any other river?**

a) The Thames   **b)** The Rhine   **c)** The Danube

3. **What is the longest river in the UK?**

a) The Thames
b) The Severn
c) The Avon

Fun and Games

1. **Which of these games involves throwing a small hoop a certain distance and trying to land it on a spike positioned on the ground?**

a) Quoits   b) Boules   c) Skittles

2. **Which piece on a chess board can move only diagonally?**

a) Knight   b) Bishop   c) Queen

3. **Monopoly games were sent to allied prisoners of war during World War II with money, maps and compasses hidden inside to help them escape. True or false?**

Mirror Match

Only one of the labelled images on this page is an exact mirror image of this cat – all of the rest have small differences.

Can you work out which cat is the exact mirror image?

a)

b)

c)

d)

e)

Spot the Difference: Alien Adventures

Answers on page 90

There are nine differences to spot between these two images. Can you find them all?

Gross and Gruesome: True or False

Can you work out which of these statements are true or false?

1. Mary Shelley, the author of *Frankenstein*, kept her dead husband's heart wrapped in silk in her desk to remember him by.

2. Henry VIII used one of his beheaded wife's heads as a football in Hampton Court.

3. A 2012 science study of 60 people's belly buttons found over 2,000 different species of bacteria living in them.

Answers on page 91

Riddle Time: Who Am I?

Can you find the answer to this riddle
using the clues on each line?

My first is in STOVE but not in OVENS,

My second is in REVERSE and also in BRING,

My third is in THATCH but not in CHEST,

My fourth is in CHAIN and also in PRISM,

My fifth is in TENT but not in BEST.

What am I?
Turn the book upside-down for a hint . . .

I am a method of transport.

Don't Sweat It!

1. **What part of your body can produce up to half a litre of sweat in just one day?**

   a) Your neck   **b)** Your forehead   **c)** Your feet

2. **Some people's sweat is coloured blue or green. True or false?**

3. **The ancient Greeks harvested sweat to flavour olive oil. True or false?**

4. **There's a competition in the USA called the Rotten Sneaker Contest for the young person with the sweatiest, stinkiest shoes. True or false?**

Answers on page 91

Make a Match: Animal Magic

Can you match each of the animals on the left with the correct fact from the right that describes it? Each fact matches with exactly one animal.

Zebra   I am the fastest land mammal.

Cheetah   I can move nearly as fast as an F1 car.

Earthworm   I can weigh around as much as ten men.

Peregrine falcon   My black-and-white markings are unique to me.

Dolphin   I am covered in tiny hairs that help me move around underground.

Polar bear   I move around in a group called a 'pod'.

Mind Your Language

1. Which country, found in the Pacific Ocean north of Australia, is home to over 800 different languages?

a) Belgium
b) Malaysia
c) Papua New Guinea

2. We get the word 'alphabet' from the first two letters of which language?

a) Chinese   b) Greek   c) French

3. **Which of these groups of countries has French as an official language in all three of the countries named?**

a) Belgium, New Zealand, Norway
b) Canada, Luxembourg, Senegal
c) South Africa, Brazil, Portugal

4. **The Khmer language (spoken in Cambodia) has an alphabet that contains the same number of letters as the English alphabet. True or false?**

Answers on page 92

Sharks: True or False

Can you work out which of these four statements
about sharks are true or false?

1. **Some sharks get through more than 35,000 teeth
    during their whole lifetime, through the natural
    process of growing them and wearing them out.**

2. **More people die from shark attacks than
    from vending machine accidents each year.**

3. **The great white shark is the biggest
    shark alive today.**

4. **There were sharks on
    the planet long before
    there were dinosaurs.**

Answers on page 92

Brilliant Birds

Can you put these birds in order of the size of their wingspan, from largest to smallest?

Bee hummingbird

Canada goose

Mallard duck

Bald eagle

Wandering albatross

House sparrow

Answers on page 93

The Amazing Amazon

1. The Amazon rainforest is nearly double the size of which country?

a) India   **b)** Switzerland   **c)** Australia

2. Over 1,000 rivers and large streams run into the Amazon river. True or false?

3. The Amazon is twice as long as any other river in the world. True or false?

Answers on page 93

Anagrams: Elephants

These **five elephant body parts** have all had their letters muddled up. Can you unscramble the capital letters on each line to reveal the part of an elephant that completes the sentence?

An elephant can use its IALT to swat flies.

Elephant SERA are very large to help them release heat from their bodies.

Elephant SUTKS are sometimes illegally sold for ivory.

An elephant uses its NUKTR to drink, breathe and smell.

An elephant's ARNIB weighs around three times as much as a human's!

Answers on page 94

Eye Eye!

I. **What is the name given to the coloured ring in your eye, surrounding your pupil?**

a) Cornea   **b)** Iris   **c)** Retina

2. **Which creature, also known as a caribou, has eyes that change colour from gold in summer to blue in winter?**

a) Reindeer
b) Guinea pigs
c) Foxes

3. **Human babies see the colour red before they are able to see the colour blue or yellow. True or false?**

Answers on page 94

What's in a Word?

Can you take a guess at what the real meaning of each of these unusual words is?

I. What is a googol?

a) The number one, followed by 100 zeros
b) A rare type of tiny spider
c) A small, dim galaxy in space

2. If you suffer from triskaidekaphobia, what do you have a deep fear of?

a) Ticks and dust mites
b) The number 13
c) Being hit by a meteorite

3. Which metal is named after the German word for goblin?

a) Nickel
b) Cobalt
c) Aluminium

Change a Letter: From Birds to Buildings

Altering just one single letter can create a word with a whole new meaning. Can you change a single letter in each of the following words to transform it into a different word, which answers the clue below it?

1. CROP
Something an axe might do

2. GREAT
Something special you might do for yourself or a friend

3. SHOCK
A rickety building

4. FLASK
A bright burst of light

5. STORM
A type of bird

6. SLIMMING
A sport

Scary Creatures

1. **What spider, named after a biblical giant, has a legspan of around 28cm and is big enough to fill a large dinner plate?**

a) Giant house spider
b) Wolf spider
c) Goliath birdeater

2. **Which creature makes its home in the Colombian rainforest, and contains enough venom to kill ten adult humans?**

a) Golden poison frog
b) Toxic lloris
c) Duck-billed platypus

3. **As well as being able to catch prey by suffocating, the anaconda has the longest fangs of any snake. True or false?**

Answers on page 95

Solar System

I. **How many planets are there in our Solar System (excluding dwarf planets)?**

a) Five   **b)** Eight   **c)** Eleven

2. **The planet Uranus has moons named Titania, Desdemona, Oberon, Puck and Ariel, among others. These are all named after characters from the plays of which writer?**

a) William Shakespeare
b) Charles Dickens
c) Roald Dahl

3. **Mercury is the closest planet to the Sun in our Solar System, yet there is evidence of ice on its surface. True or false?**

Follow the Line: Disorganized Divas

These singers have got their microphone leads in a tangle! Can you follow the lines to work out which microphone belongs with which singer?

Missing Words: Find the Time

Each of these amazing facts on the next page is missing a single word, to do with time. Can you select the one correct word from the list below to complete each of the five facts? To make it harder, there are two words that do not fit in any of the sentences.

Minutes

Milliseconds

Hours

Seconds

Decade

Day

Year

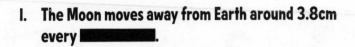

1. The Moon moves away from Earth around 3.8cm every ▮▮▮▮▮▮.

2. The shortest recorded war, the Anglo-Zanzibar war, lasted less than 45 ▮▮▮▮▮▮.

3. The first flight by an aircraft lasted 12 ▮▮▮▮▮▮.

4. Around 385,000 babies are born worldwide every ▮▮▮▮▮▮.

5. The first moonwalk by an astronaut, Neil Armstrong, lasted 2 ½ ▮▮▮▮▮▮.

Answers on page 95

SOLUTIONS

Page 5: Spot the Pair: Terrific Tigers

The matching image is **b**.

Page 6: Human Body

1. c **2.** c **3.** b

Page 7: Anagrams: Football

In the order they appear, the football terms are:
GROUND
OFFSIDE
ATTACK
LINE
INTERNATIONAL
EXTRA TIME

The first letter of each word spells out GOALIE!

Page 8: Long Lunch

1. 204m. To be precise, the hot dog measured 203.8m!
The solution to the maths puzzle is as follows:

50
x2 = 100
−20 = 80
−8 = 72
÷12 = 6
−4 = 2
x100 = 200
+4 = 204

2. 2,047. To be precise, it measured 2,047.47m
– that's around 20 football pitches in length!
The solution to the maths puzzle is as follows:

17
−2 = 15
÷3 = 5
x4 = 20
x 100 = 2,000
+50 = 2,050
−3 = 2,047

BONUS SIDE ORDER:
1. True
2. False. One pizza made in 2021 had 834 types of cheese!

Page 10: Children's Classics

1. a
2. b
3. a
4. Hans Christian Andersen

Page 11: Coral Reef Maze

Page 12: It's Pants!

1. 25m. To be precise, the underpants were 25.36m, measured across the waistband. The solution to the brain chain is as follows:

6
+9 = 15
÷3 = 5
−2 = 3
x5 = 15
+10 = 25

2. 266. That's a lot of laundry!
The solution to the maths puzzle is as follows:

16
x2 = 32
+8 = 40
x10 = 400
÷2 = 200
+70 = 270
−4 = 266

BONUS QUESTION: False

Page 14: Musical Mischief

1. b   **3.** False

2. a   **4.** True

Page 15: Broken Pieces

The two pieces that fit together are **f** and **g**.

Page 16: Toilet Time

1. b   **2.** True   **3.** a

Page 17: Riddle Time: Who Am I?

Night. The clues refer to the letters within the words on each line. For example, 'my first' refers to the first letter of the solution, 'N', which can be found in both the words 'fi_n_ger' and 'ha_n_d'. If you follow the clues down the list in the same way, you can spell out 'night', a time when you usually sleep.

Page 18: Magical Myths

1. b   **2.** a   **3.** a

Page 19: Anagrams: Solar System

In the order they appear, the words are:
MARS
VENUS
METEOROID
SATURN
NEPTUNE
ASTEROID

Page 20: Unusual World

1. c   **2.** c   **3.** True

Page 21: History: True or False

1. True
2. False
3. True
4. False. He led the first expedition that sailed around the world, but died before finishing the voyage.
5. True

Page 22: Creatures: True or False

1. False. Their blood is actually blue!
2. True
3. False
4. True

Page 23: Riddle Time!

1. They are both the same weight!
2. A cold
3. A stool
4. All of them!
5. An envelope

Page 24: Dinner Time

1. c
2. True
3. True. The banquet is held to celebrate the many monkeys who live in the town, and are thought to bring good luck.

Page 25: Make a Match: Sporting Stars

Serena Williams (Tennis)
Mo Farah (Long-distance running)
Lewis Hamilton (F1 driving)
Naomi Osaka (Tennis)
Tom Daley (Diving)
Usain Bolt (Sprinting)
Simone Biles (Gymnastics)

Page 26: Missing Words: From Spiders to Space

1. Blue
2. Strongest
3. Red
4. Longest
5. Brightest
6. Green

Page 28: Jigsaw: Cake Shop

The correct pieces are **h** and **d**. The completed jigsaw is shown above.

Page 30: Awesome Astronomy

1. a

2. b

3. True. It is a dust cloud named Sagittarius B2, that contains the same chemical found in raspberries that gives them their distinct taste.

Page 31: Change a Letter: From Cooking to Creatures

1. Change 'O' to 'A' to make 'CAT'
2. Change 'A' to 'O' to make 'MOTHS'
3. Change 'G' to 'B' to make 'BUTTER'
4. Change 'R' to 'D' to make 'FLOOD'
5. Change 'F' to 'S' to make 'SLEET'
6. Change 'S' to 'R' to make 'BARK'

Page 32: Pirate Maze

Page 33: Rugby Fun

1. c   **2.** b   **3.** c

Page 34-35: Missing Numbers

1. 5   **3.** 30   **5.** 775

2. 8   **4.** 50   **6.** 6,514

Page 36: Follow the Line: Puzzled Pilots

1 with **c**, **2** with **b**, **3** with **a**, **4** with **d**

Page 37: Movie Matters

1. c   **2.** a   **3.** True

Page 38: Waterfalls

1. b

2. True. The colour occurs because of minerals in the water.

3. True. Her name was Annie Edson Taylor, and she completed the feat in 1901.

Page 39: Change a Letter: From Plants to Places

1. Change 'P' to 'M' to make 'HOME'
2. Change 'M' to 'V' to make 'CHIVE'
3. Change 'B' to 'F' to make 'FOXES'
4. Change 'M' to 'F' to make 'FASTER'
5. Change 'T' to 'B' to make 'BRAIN'
6. Change 'N' to 'R' to make 'CLEARING'

Page 40: Computer Gaming

1. a   **2.** b   **3.** b

Page 41: Odd One Out: Fearless Flyers

The odd one out is **c**.

Page 42: Fears and Phobias

1. a   **2.** b   **3.** c

Page 43: Anagrams: Emotions

In the order they appear, the emotions are:
HAPPINESS
SADNESS
ANGER
DISGUST
EXCITEMENT
CONFUSION

Page 44: Ancient Egypt

1. c **3.** a

2. True **4.** b

Page 45: Riddle Time: Who Am I?

Skirt. The clues refer to the letters within the words on each line. For example, 'my first' refers to the first letter of the solution, 'S', which can be found in both the words 's̲ight' and 's̲mell'. If you follow the clues down the list in the same way, you can spell out 'skirt', something you can wear.

Page 46: Peculiar Plants

1. a

2. c

3. True. The plant is shaped specially to encourage shrews to poo into it. The plants get special nutrients from the poo!

Page 47: Super Science

1. b   **2.** c   **3.** a

Page 48: Smelly Stuff

1. c   **2.** True   **3.** c

Page 49: Famous Figures

From oldest to most recent, the famous figures should be ordered as follows:

Cleopatra VII (69/70–30BCE)
Joan of Arc (1412–1431)
Leonardo da Vinci (1452–1519)
William Shakespeare (1564–1616)
Marie Curie (1867–1934)
Maya Angelou (1928–2014)

Page 50: Ingenious Engines – True or False

1. True

2. True

3. False – however, there have been other speedy household appliances. In 2011, a motorized sofa became the fastest of its type when it raced at speeds of 163km/h in Australia.

Page 51: Waterways

1. c

2. c

3. b

Page 52: Fun and Games

1. a   **3.** True

2. b

Page 53: Mirror Match

The correct answer is **d**.

Page 54: Spot the Difference: Alien Adventures

Page 56: Gross and Gruesome: True or False

1. True
2. False
3. True. The study actually found 2,368 different types!

Page 57: Riddle Time: Who Am I?

Train. The clues refer to the letters within the words on each line. For example, 'my first' refers to the first letter of the solution, 'T', which can be found in the word 's<u>t</u>ove' but not in 'ovens'. If you follow the clues down the list in the same way, you can spell out 'train', a method of transport.

Page 58: Don't Sweat It!

1. c
2. True. This happens because of a rare condition called Chromhidrosis.
3. False
4. True

Page 59: Make a Match: Animal Magic

Zebra – My black-and-white markings are unique to me.
Cheetah – I am the fastest land mammal.
Earthworm – I am covered in tiny hairs that help me move around underground.
Peregrine Falcon – I can move nearly as fast as an F1 car.
Dolphin – I move around in a group called a 'pod'.
Polar Bear – I can weigh around as much as ten men.

Page 60: Mind Your Language

1. c
2. b. The first two letters of the Greek alphabet are 'alpha' and 'beta'.
3. b
4. False. The Khmer language actually has 74 letters, including some that are no longer used.

Page 62: Sharks: True or False

1. True
2. False
3. False – the whale shark is around twice as big.
4. True – the first sharks evolved around 450 million years ago. The oldest dinosaurs emerged around 200 million years later.

Page 63: Brilliant Birds

In order from the largest to the smallest wingspan,
the birds are:
Wandering albatross (around 3.4m)
Bald eagle (around 2.5m)
Canada goose (around 2m)
Mallard duck (around 95cm)
House sparrow (around 25cm)
Bee hummingbird (around 3cm)

The wandering albatross has the biggest wingspan of any
bird – it can be around 3.4m, longer than a ping pong table!

Page 64: The Amazing Amazon

1. a
2. True. It's actually around 1,100!
3. False. The Nile (found in north-east Africa) is
the longest river in the world.

Page 65: Anagrams: Elephants

In the order they appear, the parts of an elephant are:
TAIL
EARS
TUSKS
TRUNK
BRAIN

Page 66: Eye Eye!

1. b   **2.** a   **3.** True

Page 67: What's in a Word?

1. a   **2.** b   **3.** b

Page 68: Change a Letter: From Birds to Buildings

1. Change 'R' to 'H' to make 'CHOP'
2. Change 'G' to 'T' to make 'TREAT'
3. Change 'O' to 'A' to make 'SHACK'
4. Change 'K' to 'H' to make 'FLASH'
5. Change 'M' to 'K' to make 'STORK'
6. Change 'L' to 'W' to make 'SWIMMING'

Page 69: Scary Creatures

1. c
2. a
3. False. The Gaboon viper has the longest fangs. They can be up to 4cm long!

Page 70: Solar System

1. b   **2.** a   **3.** True

Page 71: Follow the Line: Disorganized Divas

1 with **c**, **2** with **a**, **3** with **b**, **4** with **d**.

Page 72: Missing Words: Find the Time

1. Year
2. Minutes
3. Seconds
4. Day
5. Hours

Try the rest of the series to carry on the fun!